W9-CEV-595

Bullard Sanford
Memorial Library
520 W. Huron Ave.
Vassar, MI 48768

ENDANGERED ANIMALS OF
EUROPE

WORLD
BOOK

a Scott Fetzer company
Chicago
worldbook.com

Staff

Executive Committee

President
Donald D. Keller
Vice President and Editor in Chief
Paul A. Kobasa
Vice President, Sales
Sean Lockwood
Vice President, Finance
Anthony Doyle
Director, Marketing
Nicholas A. Fryer
Director, Human Resources
Bev Ecker

Editorial

Associate Director,
Annuals and Topical Reference
Scott Thomas
Managing Editor,
Annuals and Topical Reference
Barbara A. Mayes
Senior Editor,
Annuals and Topical Reference
Christine Sullivan
Manager, Indexing Services
David Pofelski
Administrative Assistant
Ethel Matthews
Manager, Contracts & Compliance
(Rights & Permissions)
Loranne K. Shields

Editorial Administration

Senior Manager, Publishing
Operations
Timothy Falk

Manufacturing/ Production

Director
Carma Fazio
Manufacturing Manager
Sandra Johnson
Production/Technology
Manager
Anne Fritzinger
Proofreader
Nathalie Strassheim

Graphics and Design

Art Director
Tom Evans
Senior Designer
Don Di Sante
Media Researcher
Jeff Heimsath
Manager, Cartographic Services
Wayne K. Pichler
Senior Cartographer
John M. Rejba

Marketing

Marketing Specialists
Alannah Sharry
Annie Suhy
Digital Marketing Specialists
Iris Liu
Nudrat Zoha

Writer

A. J. Smuskiewicz

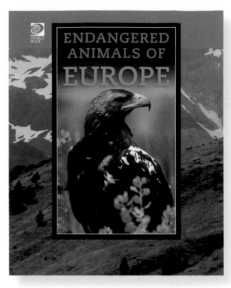

The cover image is the endangered Spanish imperial eagle.

Copyright © 2015 World Book Inc. All rights reserved.

This volume may not be reproduced in whole or in part in any form without written permission from the publisher. WORLD BOOK and the GLOBE DEVICE are registered trademarks or trademarks of World Book, Inc.

World Book, Inc.
233 North Michigan Avenue
Chicago, Illinois 60601 U.S.A.

For information about other World Book publications, visit our website at **www.worldbook.com** or call **1-800-WORLDBK (967-5325).**
For information about sales to schools and libraries, call 1-800-975-3250 (United States) or 1-800-837-5365 (Canada).

Library of Congress Cataloging-in-Publication Data

Endangered animals of Europe.
    pages cm -- (Endangered animals of the world)
  Summary: "Information about some of the more important and interesting endangered animals of Europe, including the animal's common name, scientific name, and conservation status; also includes a map showing the range of each animal featured; and a glossary, additional resources, and an index"-- Provided by publisher.
  Includes index.
  ISBN 978-0-7166-5624-1
  1. Endangered species--Europe--Juvenile literature. 2. Wildlife conservation--Europe--Juvenile literature. 3. Extinction (Biology)-- Juvenile literature. I. World Book, Inc.
  QH77.E85E53 2015
  591.68094--dc23

                                                    2014019664

Endangered Animals of the World
ISBN: 978-0-7166-5620-3 (set)

Printed in China by Shenzhen Donnelley Printing Co., Ltd. Guangdong Province
1st printing October 2014

Contents

Why species in Europe are threatened

Europe's wildlife has long struggled with threats from the continent's human population. People began arriving in Europe, one of the world's smallest continents, more than 700,000 years ago. By the end of prehistoric times—about 3000 B.C.—farming had spread to all parts of the continent, except the dense northern forests. Over the following centuries, major cities, little towns, factories and other businesses, ranches, and roads covered the continent.

Although recent population growth has greatly slowed, Europe today averages about 180 people per square mile (70 people per square kilometer). That makes Europe the second most densely populated continent, after Asia. Europe is three times as densely populated as North America.

The result of this population pressure has been centuries of overhunting, overfishing, destruction of *habitats* (living areas), chemical pollution, and other environmentally harmful activities. Numerous native animal *species* have been wiped out. (A species is a group of plants or animals that have certain permanent characteristics in common and are able to interbreed.) The populations of some species, including the wild Mediterranean monk seal and Spanish (Iberian) lynx, have been reduced to hundreds of individuals.

Today, roughly 25 percent of Europe's animal species—some 2,800 kinds of animal—are threatened with extinction, according to a 2011 report by the European Union (EU, a partnership of many European countries). The report was based on studies of thousands of species by the International Union for Conservation of Nature (IUCN), a global organization of conservation groups.

Of course, this number includes only those known to science. Some species remain undiscovered. And almost certainly, a number of these animals are in peril or have even disappeared.

Threats. Human *development* (activities) has squeezed Europe's forests, grasslands, and other natural habitats into smaller and smaller *fragments* (pieces). The result has been a huge drop in the continent's *biodiversity* (the variety that exists among different types of animals and plants, including differences in species). "Biodiversity is in crisis, with species extinctions running at unparalleled rates," the EU report stated.

Europe's wildlife have also suffered from the introduction, by people, of plant and animal species into Europe that threaten native species. A more recent threat is global warming, a phenomenon caused mainly by human activities, which could threaten the survival of many species in the cold regions of Europe, including the high Alps.

Conservation. Two of Europe's most important conservation plans are called the Habitats Directive and the Birds Directive. These plans require EU countries to guarantee the protection of endangered species and the conservation of the species's main breeding and resting sites.

Saving endangered species is possible. The European bison, also called the wisent, is one critically endangered species that has been pulled back from the edge of extinction.

Scientific sequence. The species described in this book are presented in a standard scientific sequence that generally goes from simple to complex. This sequence starts with *invertebrates* (animals without backbones) and then moves through fish, reptiles, birds, and mammals.

Range. The red areas on maps indicate an animal's *range* (area in which it naturally occurs) on the European continent.

Glossary: Italicized words, except for scientific names, appear with their definitions in the Glossary at the end of the book.

Conservation status. Each species discussed in this book is listed with its common name, scientific name, and conservation status. The conservation status tells how seriously a species is threatened. Unless noted differently, the status is according to the International Union for Conservation of Nature (IUCN), a global organization of conservation groups. The most serious IUCN status is *Extinct,* followed by *Extinct in the Wild, Critically Endangered, Endangered, Vulnerable, Near Threatened,* and *Least Concern.* Criteria used to determine these conservation statuses are included in the chart to the right.

Conservation statuses

Extinct All individuals of the species have died

Extinct in the Wild The species is no longer observed in its past range

Critically Endangered The species will become extinct unless immediate conservation action is taken

Endangered The species is at high risk of becoming extinct due to a large decrease in range, population, or both

Vulnerable The species is at some risk of becoming extinct due to a moderate decrease in range, population or both

Near Threatened The species is likely to become threatened in the future

Least Concern The species is common throughout its range

Icons. The icons indicate various threats that have made animals vulnerable to extinction.

Key to icons

 Disease

 Global warming

 Habitat disturbance

 Habitat loss

 Hunting

 Overfishing

 Pet trade

 Pollution

Carabus olympiae

Conservation status: Vulnerable

Carabus olympiae, sometimes known as Olimpe's ground beetle, is one of hundreds of *species* (types) of ground beetles in Europe. Many of the beetles have brilliant iridescent coloring. That is, their rainbowlike colors of metallic green, gold, and purple change, depending on the angle at which you view them.

The beetles may look beautiful to people, but to snails and other small *invertebrates* (animals without backbones), they are a terror. Adult *C. olympiae* and their wormlike *larvae* (immature forms) attack and eat large numbers of invertebrates.

C. olympiae grows to a length of 1 1/2 inches (3.8 centimeters). People usually see the beetle at night, especially during periods of heavy rains and high humidity.

Habitat and threats. *C. olympiae* is known in only one small area of forest and shrubland, high in the Italian Alps. Lifts, runs, and roads associated with the skiing industry have destroyed much of the beetle's natural *habitat* (living area).

Carabo beetle

Collectors and grazing cattle also pose a serious threat. Attempts to introduce *C. olympiae* to the French Alps have been unsuccessful.

Carabus olympiae, **which lives only in a small area of the Italian Alps, is prized by collectors for its brilliant coloring.**

Great raft spider

Dolomedes plantarius

Conservation status: Vulnerable

With a body length of about 0.8 inch (2 centimeters)—not counting its legs—the great raft spider is one of the largest spiders in Europe. Its name comes from its ability to "walk on water." The spider waits for prey by sitting on a plant growing above the surface of a marsh, fen, or other body of water. Its back legs are on the plant, and its front legs touch the water surface. When its front legs sense the vibrations of an insect, fish, other spider, or other small animal, the spider runs across the water to capture the prey. It can also crawl down the plant and into the water to catch prey.

Great raft spider

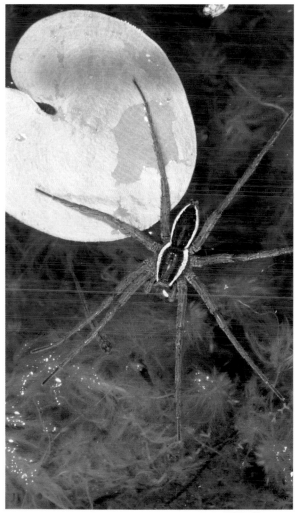

Reproduction. Male and female great raft spiders mate on the surface of the water. The male slowly approaches the female by first tapping his front feet on the water surface. The female may tap back. If the vibrations suggest that she is friendly, he will row or run to her and begin mating.

The female produces hundreds of eggs inside a silk sac. She attaches the sac to a tentlike web that she builds on a plant sticking above the water surface. After the spiderlings hatch from the eggs, she protects them for several days until they go off on their own.

Habitat. Great raft spiders are found in many European countries, though their numbers have fallen significantly since the mid-1900's because of the destruction of their *habitat* (living area). The spiders need still or slowly moving water in *wetlands* (water-soaked land), many of which have been drained to provide water for the public. Wetlands have also been turned into farmland or *degraded* (reduced in quality) by chemical pollution.

The great raft spider has been threatened by the loss of its wetland habitats.

Margaritifera margaritifera

Conservation status: Endangered

The freshwater pearl mussel is one of the world's longest-lived *invertebrates* (animals with backbones). If the mussel survives its first year, it can live from 86 to 102 years in the wild. (Scientists determine the age of a mussel by measuring its size.) Scientists found one mussel that was 280 years old!

Habitat. Freshwater pearl mussels live buried in the sandy bottoms of rivers and streams in *habitats* (living areas) ranging from western Europe and the United Kingdom to the Ural Mountains of Russia. People have also brought this species to the northeastern United States and eastern Canada.

Appearance. The freshwater pearl mussel is a *mollusk* (soft-bodied animal with a hard shell). Mussels actually have two long shells that are hinged together on one side. The shells grow as the animal ages, changing from yellowish brown to black. The outer surfaces of older parts of the shells appear rough and worn-out. The insides are lined with a shiny, smooth, and pearly material. This rainbow-colored material, called mother-of-pearl, is often used in jewelry.

Reproduction. Freshwater pearl mussels have an unusual reproduction cycle. Male mussels release their *sperm* (male sex cells) in the water near waiting females. The females inhale the sperm, which then fertilize their *eggs* (female sex cells). The fertilized eggs grow in a special sac in the female's body. After several weeks, the female ejects millions of *larvae* (immature forms) measuring only 0.04 to 0.08 inch (1 to 2 millimeters) in the water. Many of the larvae are swept away by river currents. Many others become tasty morsels for fish and other aquatic animals.

To survive, the tiny mussels must be inhaled by an Atlantic salmon, sea trout, or similar fish. Once inside, the larvae snap their tiny shells

Freshwater pearl mussel

The freshwater pearl mussel is threatened by damage to its watery habitat by pollution and dam construction.

shut on the fish's gills. There the larvae take in oxygen and grow.

Some months later, the larvae drop off the gills to settle on the gravelly or sandy stream bottom. The mussels partially bury themselves there, anchoring themselves with a large, muscular foot. They feed on tiny debris that drifts down through the water. This debris consists of particles from plants or animals, including pieces of dead, decayed bodies. If the mussels survive to adulthood there, they may reach a size of 6 inches (15 centimeters) or more.

Threats. Freshwater pearl mussels were once among the most common mollusks in Europe. However, the population of this species has declined greatly, and it is now extinct in many parts of its former *range* (area in which it naturally occurs). The main reasons for the decline are such human activities as river pollution, dam construction, drainage projects, and *dredging* (clearing out the bottom of rivers or other bodies of water so that ships can navigate easily). Drops in the numbers of native salmon and trout species have also harmed the freshwater pearl mussel, because the mussel larvae need these species during their early growth phase.

Conservation. Conservationists are trying to protect the freshwater pearl mussel by reintroducing adult mussels to areas where the species has become extinct. But the most important conservation action is working to restore *degraded* (damaged) river habitats to more natural conditions.

Angel shark

Squatina squatina
Conservation status: Critically Endangered

This shark is usually not a threat to people. But if disturbed, it will quickly deliver a painful bite with its strong jaws and needlelike teeth. The IUCN has classified the angel shark as one of the 100 most threatened species on Earth.

Appearance. Like other sharks, the angel shark has a boneless skeleton. The skeleton is made of a tough, elastic substance called cartilage. But the angel shark does not look like a typical shark. It has a flattened body and wide *pectoral* (shoulder) *fins* that make it look a little like a ray or a skate. Its skin is grey to reddish or greenish-brown, with scattered small, white spots and blackish dots.

Like a catfish, the angel shark has long whiskerlike growths, called *barbels*, near its nose. These growths help the shark feel its way around in the dark during its nighttime hunts for prey.

Compared with many other shark species, the angel shark is relatively small. Females, which are larger than males, may reach a length of almost 8 feet (2.4 meters) and a weight of 176 pounds (80 kilograms). The largest females tend to have the largest number of young, giving birth to as many as 25 young at a time.

Hunting. Angel sharks hunt in two ways. During the daytime, they bury their flat bodies in the muddy or sandy sea bottom. Only their eyes stick out to search for passing prey. If a fish, *mollusk* (soft-bodied marine animal), or *crustacean* swims by, the sharks will quickly dart out to grab it with their strong jaws. (A crustacean is an *invertebrate* [animal without a backbone] with many jointed legs and a hard external shell.) The sharks' favorite food seems to be bony fish, particularly flatfish. During the night, the sharks usually hunt by swimming around in search of their prey.

Angel shark

Habitat. The angel shark lives in the northeastern Atlantic Ocean, from the waters of Norway and Sweden to those of the United Kingdom. Its *habitat* (living area) also includes the Mediterranean and Black seas. The shark sometimes swims into *brackish* (slightly salty) waters, such as at river mouths. During the cold, winter months, many angel sharks move south to warmer waters.

Threats. People have been catching angel sharks for thousands of years. The fish are prized for their meat and their rough skin, which is used for polishing wood.

Since the mid-1900's, however, the number of angel sharks has fallen drastically, mainly because of certain practices of the fishing industry. Both immature and adult angel sharks are often accidentally captured and killed in large nets used in *trawling* for tuna and other commercial fish. In trawling, a net is pulled through the water behind a boat. As a result, angel sharks have become extinct in much of their original *range* (area in which they occur naturally) in the northeastern Atlantic and Mediterranean.

Fishing is not the only threat to this species. Angel sharks have also become endangered because of habitat disturbances from pollution and tourist activities.

Conservation. Angel sharks gained some measure of protection within their range with the establishment of three marine reserves around the Balearic Islands. This group of islands lies east of the mainland of Spain in the Mediterranean Sea.

The angel shark is often caught and killed accidentally by fishers seeking other kinds of fish.

Anguilla anguilla

Conservation status: Critically endangered

The European eel is also known as the "common" eel. This *species* (type) of snakelike fish used to be extremely common in almost all European rivers draining into the Mediterranean Sea and the North and Baltic seas. It was also common in much of the northern and central Atlantic Ocean. But the European eel is no longer common and is, in fact, in great danger of extinction. For many reasons, the population of the European eel is in a steep decline.

Appearance. European eels are relatively small compared with other species of eels. Females are typically larger than males. The longest recorded length for a female is 4.4 feet (1.3 meters).

Life cycle. European eels breed in the sea—especially the Sargasso Sea in the west-central Atlantic—but they spend most of the rest of their lives in fresh water. The female eel lays her *eggs* (female sex cells) in the sea in the spring before she dies. Each egg hatches into a tiny, narrow *larva* (immature form). As ocean currents carry the larvae northward, they undergoes a *metamorphosis* (change in body form) and develop into miniature, transparent forms called glass eels. At this stage, they are highly sought for a Japanese food called sushi.

The color of the European eel changes as it grows and gets older. By the time the glass eels reach the coast of Europe, they have developed some coloration and are known as elvers. Scientists believe that male elvers stay in salt water along the coast. Most female elvers swim into rivers and other bodies of fresh water.

When the eels become sexually mature, they become a silvery color. As they continue to age, they take on a yellowish, brownish, or greenish color. Some European eels have been known to live as long as 85 years, but most do not live that long in the wild.

European eel

Amazingly, these eels can survive on land for several hours, if conditions are moist. That means that they can squirm across land from one body of water to another, particularly on rainy nights when the ground is wet.

Threats. The population of the European eel has fallen greatly since the 1960's—though scientists do not fully understand all the reasons for this decline. One reason is surely the killing of young eels for sushi. Another reason is likely the construction on rivers of hydroelectric dams, whose fast-spinning turbines kill eels swimming near them.

Another eel threat is chemical pollution of their aquatic *habitats* (living areas) from agricultural and industrial sources. A number of European eels have also died from infection by a *nematode* (roundworm) parasite. That parasitic worm was carried to the European eels' habitats by eels introduced from Japan by people.

To save this species from extinction, conservationists have called for a greater effort to protect and manage eel populations and the eel's natural habitats.

The once-common European eel is disappearing from much of its former *range* (the region in which certain plants and animals occur naturally).

Proteus anguinus

Conservation status: Vulnerable

The olm, also known as the proteus, is an extremely unusual amphibian. It is the only *vertebrate* (animal with backbone) in Europe that has adapted to living in caves. Specifically, it lives in cool bodies of water inside underground caves in central Europe.

Appearance. The olm's transparent, pinkish-white skin is one of the strangest things about this animal: Its internal organs can be seen through the skin. Also very strange are the olm's four thin, little legs, which look somewhat like human arms with tiny hands. Another name for the olm is "the human fish." That is because some people think the olm looks like a weird, little, naked human swimming in the water. The olm has three bright pink gills on each side of its head. It typically grows to a length of about 9.8 inches (25 centimeters).

Lifespan. Biologists believe that the average lifespan of these creatures is about 70 years and that some individuals may survive more than 100 years. This lifespan makes the olm the longest-living known amphibian species.

Hunting and diet. In the darkness of caves, vision is useless. And in fact, the olm's tiny eyes cannot see other objects or their surroundings. To hunt, the olm uses its sharp senses of taste, hearing, and smell. It can also sense the movements of other creatures in the water. Its prey include insect *larvae* (immature forms) and small *mollusks* (soft-bodied animals) and *crustaceans (*hard-shelled animals).

However, not being able to find a meal may not be much of a problem for an animal that has been called a "master of starvation." Studies with captive olms have shown that the animals can go for 10 years without eating! During such periods, olms actually reabsorb their own body tissues.

Olm (Proteus)

Breeding. Olm do not become sexually mature until they are about 12 years old. When breeding season arrives, each male sets up a *territory* (personal area) into which he admits only females. After he mates with a female and she lays her eggs under a rock or other hiding place, he may help her guard the eggs until they hatch. Not all females lay eggs. Some give birth to live young.

Threats. Most olms live in countries along the Adriatic Sea, including in far-northern Italy, Slovenia, Croatia, and Bosnia and Herzegovina. Populations of the animals in this region are *fragmented* (broken up) and isolated from each other. The watery cave *habitats* (living areas) of olms have been greatly disturbed by human activities. For example, when homes, businesses, or farms are built on land near the water systems in which olms live, underground water levels may fall as water is pumped to the surface for people's use. *Toxic* (poisonous) pollution from factories, farms, and waste dumps may make the underground water uninhabitable for olms.

Another threat is the collection of olms for sale as pets, laboratory animals, and even pig food. Although governments in the Adriatic region have passed laws to protect the olm, these laws are not always enforced.

The olm is a cave-dwelling amphibian. If left undisturbed by human activities, it may live for 100 years.

Meadow viper *and* Caucasian viper

Vipers are *venomous* (poisonous) snakes that have a pair of long, hollow fangs in their upper jaw. They kill their prey by biting into their flesh and injecting venom through their fangs, the way a hypodermic needle injects liquid. Vipers also defend themselves this way. The venom forms in special glands in the snake's body.

Meadow (Orsini's) viper
Vipera ursinii
Conservation status: Vulnerable

The body of a meadow viper is marked by a beautiful, dark, zigzag pattern. The top of its head has a dark, V-shaped mark. This snake grows to lengths ranging from 13.8 to 23.6 inches (35 to 60 centimeters), with females usually larger than males.

Grasshoppers, crickets, beetles, rodents, lizards, and birds make up most of the diet of the meadow viper. The viper can usually kill its prey with just one bite.

Meadow (Orsini's) viper

Caucasian (Kaznakow's) viper

Once widespread, the meadow viper is believed to be extinct in Austria and Bulgaria and close to extinction in Hungary and Moldova.

Habitat. In addition to meadows, meadow vipers are found in marshy areas and rocky hillsides. Its natural *range* (extent of its area) extends from France eastward to Hungary and Romania and southward to Albania and Greece. However, many populations in this region have become extinct.

Threats. The most dangerous threat to the meadow viper is the conversion of its meadow *habitat* (living area) to agricultural land, with the heavy use of chemical pesticides and fertilizers and grazing by livestock. Roads, ski runs, and other *developments* (human activities) have also disturbed the snake's habitat. In addition, meadow vipers are sometimes trapped for sale as pets and laboratory research animals.

Caucasian (Kaznakow's) viper
Vipera kaznakovi

Conservation status: Endangered

The Caucasian viper is closely related to the meadow viper and can grow to about the same length, 23.6 inches (60 centimeters). But its coloration is different. In fact, the Caucasian viper's coloration varies greatly among individuals of the species, ranging from mostly red to mostly yellow to all black. Whatever their main

The Caucasian viper is one of the deadliest snakes in the world. But its venom has also been used for centuries to help stop bleeding.

color, all individuals have a dark stripe along the back.

Habitat. This *species* (type) can be found in countries in the Caucasus region of eastern Europe, including parts of Georgia, Russia, and Turkey. Its main habitat consists of various kinds of forests and woodlands, including *conifer* (cone-bearing tree) forests and willow forests. The vipers may even survive on land that has been cleared to plant tea and other crops.

Threats. The venom of the Caucasian viper ranks among the strongest and most dangerous snake poisons known. But medicines carefully prepared with this venom have been used for thousands of years to help stop bleeding in people. Despite this benefit, the deadliness of the viper's bite has made the viper a common target of human hunters. Capturing the snakes to sell as exotic pets has also contributed to the sharp drop in Caucasian viper populations. Another threat is the continued destruction of the viper's habitat for human developments.

Gallotia auaritae

Conservation status: Critically endangered

Fewer than 50 members of this *species* (type) may exist—if they exist at all. The lizard is native to the Canary Islands, a group of islands that make up two provinces of Spain about 60 miles (97 kilometers) off the northwest coast of Africa. Different species of giant lizards live on different islands in this group. The La Palma giant lizard was known to live in on or near the shore of the island of La Palma. Humans settled this island approximately 2,000 years ago and soon began slaughtering the lizards for food and other reasons.

Scientists thought that the La Palma giant lizard had become extinct sometime within the past few hundred years. But then in 2007, a few people reported seeing the lizard! So now many scientists believe that a small population of the reptiles may still exist on La Palma. Other scientists, however, are skeptical about the reported sightings. They doubt that any of these lizards have survived to today.

Appearance. Most of what is known about the body of this rare lizard comes from studies of fossils and skeletons kept in zoological collections. Scientists have never been able to study a living member of this species.

Biologists estimate that the La Palma giant lizard can grow to a length of about 17 inches (44 centimeters). The lizard has a sturdy body with muscular legs. Males are larger than females. According to the few recent sightings, the lizard is dark brown.

Daily life. Scientists know little about the *habits* (living areas) of the La Palma giant lizard. It's likely that, like most other lizards, the females lay eggs. From the lizard's teeth, biologists have concluded that it eats mostly plants. It probably grows slowly.

Threats. Besides being killed for human food, the La Palma giant lizard was killed by cats,

The lizard shown right in a still image from a video may be a La Palma giant lizard, long thought to be extinct. But many scientists doubt the lizard still exists. The lizard was named for the Canary Island on which it was found (below).

dogs, and other predators that were introduced to La Palma by people. The lizard was probably slow-moving and found it difficult to escape from these faster predators. Land *development* on the island—including the construction of towns and the conversion of natural habitat to cropland and grazing land—also greatly harmed the species.

Conservation. Scientists continue to try to determine if the lizard still exists. If they can prove that the lizard has survived, the scientists will need to figure out how large the population is. They will also need to establish conservation plans to make sure that the La Palma giant lizard does not really become extinct.

There are numerous *species* (types) of wall lizard in the *genus Podarcis*. (A genus is a group of closely related species.) Some species of wall lizard are considered critically endangered. Others are threatened or vulnerable. Most species of wall lizard are native to Europe and northern Africa. Some have been introduced to North America by people.

Appearance. Wall lizards generally range from less than 12 to no more than 36 inches (30 to 90 centimeters), with thin, flattened bodies that are greenish or brownish and striped or speckled. Some individuals may have marks of blue or other bright colors.

Tricky tail. The tail of a wall lizard may be twice as long as the rest of the body. The tail is an amazing defensive weapon. If an enemy seizes the tail, the tail breaks off but keeps wriggling as though it were alive. Then, while

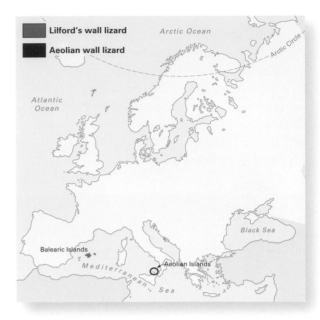

- ■ Lilford's wall lizard
- ■ Aeolian wall lizard

Arctic Ocean
Arctic Circle
Atlantic Ocean
Black Sea
Balearic Islands
Aeolian Islands
M e d i t e r r a n e a n   S e a

A Lilford's wall lizard (below) and an Aeolian wall lizard (opposite page) enjoy the heat of sun-warmed rocks.

its enemy is distracted, the lizard crawls to safety. A new tail grows, but it is a slightly different color and is not as well developed as the original.

Sunning. Wall lizards are typically inactive during the coldest periods of winter, when they shelter under rocks or in other hiding places. But they often come out to sun themselves on warmer winter days.

Diet. Wall lizards are active hunters that race across the ground in search of insects or spiders. The lizards also eat berries and other fruits.

Reproduction. The lizards mate in spring. Females may lay two or more clutches of eggs during the year.

Aeolian wall lizard
Podarcis raffonei
Conservation status: Critically Endangered

This lizard takes its name from the Aeolian Islands where it lives. These rocky islands, which were formed by volcanoes, lie off the northern coast of Sicily in the Mediterranean Sea. The lizard's preferred *habitat* (living area) consists of the natural rocky landscape or patches of shrubland.

Threats. Populations of this species have been severely affected by nonnative animals that people brought to the islands—especially other kinds of lizards that compete with Aeolian lizards for food and habitat. The lizards are also collected for sale as pets. Because their remaining populations are so small and isolated, biologists fear that they could easily become extinct as the result of a natural disaster or disease.

Lilford's wall lizard
Podarcis lilfordi
Conservation status: Critically Endangered

The Lilford's wall lizard lives in rocky areas and scrubland on the Balearic Islands, off the eastern coast of Spain.

Threats. The survival of the Lilford's wall lizard is seriously threatened by cats and other predators that people have introduced to the Balearic Islands. The lizard is also collected for the pet trade. Another threat is the poison bait people put out to kill rats and seagulls. The grazing of goats by the islands' inhabitants has also *degraded* (damaged) the lizard's habitat.

Bullard Sanford Memorial Library
520 W. Huron Ave.

Aquila adalberti

Conservation status: Vulnerable

The Spanish imperial eagle is one of the largest and most striking *raptors* (birds of prey) in Europe. The bird may grow to a length of 29 to 33 inches (75 to 84 centimeters). Its wingspan may be from about 6 to 7 feet (1.8 to 2 meters).

The Spanish imperial eagle's cream-colored head offers a handsome contrast to its dark brown body feathers. In addition to its physical appearance, the bird can be identified by its unique style of flying. It often glides flatly and evenly across the sky. It also makes a distinctive, repetitive barking call that sounds like a loud, harsh "owk owk owk."

Reproduction. Like many other kinds of raptors, male and female Spanish imperial eagles mate for life. They usually build their nests high in oak trees. Both parents *incubate* the eggs (keep them warm) and feed and protect the chicks. When the parents feed the young, they use their sharp bills and *talons* (claws) to tear the meat into small pieces.

Diet. The Spanish imperial eagle preys mainly on rabbits. In fact, the eagle is so dependent on rabbits that the bird's numbers and its ability to reproduce are directly related to the abundance of rabbits. In years when the rabbit population is low, the eagles produce relatively few eagle chicks. But in years when the rabbit population is high, there will likely be many chicks.

Habitat. The eagle can be found in the central region of Spain. It lives in a variety of *habitats* (living areas) including marshes, plains, dunes, hillsides, and mountain slopes. However, the eagles' stay in any particular area depends on whether they can capture a steady supply of rabbits. If rabbits are scarce, the eagles will fly elsewhere to seek their favorite food.

Threats. The Spanish imperial eagle is now legally protected in Spain. But biologists still fear for the long-term survival of the bird. Farming, logging, and the construction of human settlements have destroyed forests and fields where the eagle lives.

Viral diseases have killed large numbers of the rabbits on which the eagle depends for food. Poisons set out by hunters who want to prevent the eagles and other predators from killing game animals have also taken a toll. Collisions with dangerous electric power lines have claimed numerous eagles, particularly females.

Conservation. In an effort to protect the Spanish imperial eagle, some European governments have required electric companies to redesign power lines to reduce the bird's chances of being electrocuted. Scientists have also increased their efforts to protect the breeding sites, eggs, and young of the eagles. In addition, conservationists have successfully released into the wild a number young eagles bred in captivity.

Despite gaining legal protections, the Spanish imperial eagle faces serious threats to its survival.

Otis tarda

Conservation status: Vulnerable

The great bustard is one of the heaviest of all flying birds. Males grow to a a weight of about 40 pounds (18 kilograms) and a height of about 3.4 feet (1 meter). The male's wingspan may be up to 8 feet (2.5 meters) wide. Males are larger than females. Males are also more colorful, with a reddish-brown band of feathers across the breast. This band grows in size as the bird gets older.

Displays. Male great bustards perform remarkable displays to attract females. First, the males gather at display grounds, known as *leks*. Then they inflate an air sac in their neck like a big balloon. They also raise their feathers and twist their bodies into odd postures while strutting around the lek.

Reproduction. After a female selects one of the males as her mate, the two birds pair up to reproduce. She lays one to three eggs in a shallow nest that she digs into the ground. Then she sits on the eggs to *incubate* them (keep them warm) for approximately 25 days—with no help from her mate.

The young bustards grow and develop survival skills quickly. They are able to forage for insects, seeds, and other food on their own when they are only 10 days old. They can fly by the time they are about 30 days old.

Habitat. Great bustards live in a type of dry grassland and shrubland known as a *steppe*—as well as on farmland—in scattered parts of Europe and Asia, from Portugal to Turkey to China. Some populations of the birds migrate between summer breeding grounds and wintering sites.

Threats. The great bustard is vulnerable to extinction mainly as a result of changes to its *habitat* (living area). Many natural steppe grasslands and shrublands have been converted into

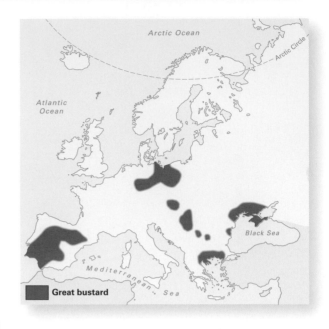

Great bustard

farms or towns. Although the bustards can survive and feed on farmland, they prefer undisturbed natural land for their leks and breeding sites. Farms that rely heavily on irrigation and large amounts of chemical fertilizers and pesticides are especially threatening to the bustard populations.

An additional threat to the bird is the construction of roads, fences, and electric power lines, with which the bustards sometimes collide. *Poachers* (people who hunt animals illegally) also kill the large birds.

Conservation. Laws and conservation programs help to protect the great bustard in many European and Asian nations. However, biologists believe that more work can be done, including restoring natural habitats, adopting less harmful farming practices, and cracking down on illegal hunting. Scientists are working to develop more effective conservation plans.

A great bustard male displays his plumage to attract a female.

Pelecanus crispus

Conservation status: Vulnerable

Silvery-white feathers and an orange-red pouch under its bill make the Dalmatian pelican quite a special-looking bird. Although these colors fade after the breeding season, the pelican remains a remarkable bird to observe.

The Dalmatian pelican is very large, sometimes reaching a length of almost 6 feet (1.8 meters). It has a wingspan of from 9 1/2 to 11 1/2 feet (3 to 3.5 meters).

The pelican is a great swimmer, spending much of its time in river deltas, coastal lagoons, marshes, and swamps. It feeds as it swims, dunking it head below the surface of the water to find fish, shrimps, insect *larvae* (immature forms), worms, and other aquatic prey to capture. The birds sometimes fish together in groups. Pelicans don't always eat the food they catch right away. They may store it in the expandable pouch to eat later.

Breeding. Dalmatian pelicans make a number of unusual sounds, including hisses, barks, and grunts. They are especially vocal during the breeding season, in spring.

The females lay two to four eggs in nests made of reeds, sticks, and other plant material. They *incubate* the eggs (keep them warm) for about a month, until they hatch. The young pelicans develop their flight feathers within approximately 80 days. They can then fly off on their own.

Habitat. The birds get their name from Dalmatia, a region of Croatia on the eastern coast of the Adriatic Sea in central Europe. Some Dalmatian pelicans breed in central or eastern Europe but spend winter a bit farther south, in the eastern part of the Mediterranean. Other Dalmatian pelicans breed in Russia and central Asia and overwinter in Iran, Iraq, or India. The largest colony of this *species* (type) is found at Lake Mikri Prespa in Greece.

Threats. Populations of Dalmatian pelicans have fallen as much of their *wetland* (water-soaked) habitat has been drained for use as farmland and other human *developments* (activities). The birds have also been shot and killed in large numbers by fishers, who view the pelicans as competitors for their own catches.

Additional threats to the birds include the depletion of their prey by fishers, pollution of their watery habitats with agricultural and industrial chemicals, and collisions with electric power lines. In Mongolia, traditional *nomadic* (wandering) herders kill the pelicans to cut off their throat pouches, which they use for carrying things.

Conservation. European conservationists have helped to slow the decline of the Dalmatian pelican. Their actions have included the construction of special platforms that the birds can use as nest sites and the removal of dangerous power lines. The most important action, however, is the protection and restoration of the birds' wetland habitats.

The Dalmatian pelican sometimes stores the food it catches in its pouch to eat later.

Lynx pardinus

Conservation status: Critically Endangered

Biologists consider the Spanish lynx, also known as the Iberian lynx, to be the most endangered *species* (type) of cat in the world. There may be fewer than 300 individuals in the wild. All live in small, isolated populations within the woodlands, scrublands, and pastures of central and southwestern Spain and parts of Portugal.

Appearance. Spanish lynx average from 39 to 48 inches (99 to 121 centimeters) long, including their black-tipped tail. They weigh from 22 to 29 pounds (10 to 13 kilograms). Their beautiful fur is basically gray in color but may also be yellowish or rust-colored. Although most lynxes have black spots covering their bodies, these spots are not always clearly visible.

Lynxes also have long tufts of fur at the tips of their pointed ears, long whiskers, and ruffs of hair around the sides of their face.

Threats. The Spanish lynx population has fallen dramatically as disease and hunting have killed off large numbers of European rabbits. The rabbits make up most, if not all, of the lynx's prey. The rabbit population has been devastated by such diseases as myxomatosis (which causes tumors and sometimes blindness and pneumonia) and rabbit hemorrhagic disease (which causes bleeding and sometimes paralysis and coma). In addition, the rabbits have been excessively hunted by people.

In addition, the natural *habitat* (living area) of the Spanish lynx has been *degraded* (damaged) and *fragmented* (broken up) by the planting of pine and eucalyptus trees on scrublands and by livestock grazing and the construction of roads, dams, and homes. Chemical pollution from farms and industries has added to these habitat problems.

Fragmentation has been particularly damaging to the Spanish lynx because different pop-

ulations of the cat have become isolated from one another. Normally, when lynx are about 20 months old, they leave their mother's area and move to new areas. But because of fragmentation, the animals may be unable to cross through *developments* (human activities) to new areas. Lynxes may thus be forced to remain in the area where they were born and may end up mating with related animals. This *inbreeding* tends to weaken a species over time, making it more vulnerable to disease and other risks that threaten its existence. Some 40 populations of Spanish lynx appear to have collapsed since the early 1980's, according to the IUCN.

Conservation. Spanish lynx have been legally protected in Spain and Portugal since the 1970's. Nevertheless, continued habitat destruction, *poaching* (illegal hunting), and other problems pose serious threats to this cat. One ray of hope is a captive-breeding program, in which lynx are being bred and raised in captivity for eventual release into the wild.

The Spanish lynx is considered the most endangered species of cat in the world.

Vormela peregusna

Conservation status: Vulnerable

The polecats of Europe and Asia are members of the weasel family that look and act somewhat like the skunks of North America. The polecat's most obvious resemblance to a skunk is the strong-smelling fluid from scent glands under its tail that it sprays when it is frightened. Getting this nasty-smelling spray on your body is very likely to persuade you to leave the animal alone. Polecats are famous for being aggressive and fearless, with other animals as well as with people. Polecats also use their scent to mark their *territory* (the area an animal defends against other animals).

European marbled polecat

Appearance. With its reddish-brown fur mottled with yellowish patches, the European marbled polecat looks less like a skunk than do other *species* (types) of polecats, which are black and white. But European marbled polecats have a skunklike mask of black fur around their eyes, in addition to a big bushy tail.

Male marbled polecats, which are larger than females, measure from 11 to 15 inches (28 to 38 centimeters) long. The tail adds another 6 to 9 inches (15 to 22 centimeters).

Hunting and breeding. A polecat's slender, short-legged body allows it to chase mice, rats, and other rodents right into their burrows. Its front paws are equipped with long, sharp claws to help it dig out the prey if necessary. Polecats may also eat eggs, birds, rabbits, reptiles, amphibians, fish, insects, and even fruit. Polecats hunt and forage for food mostly at night, using their strong sense of smell.

Polecats live alone, except during the mating season or when the female is raising her young. Five to eight young are born about 40 days after mating. The young leave their mother after about three months.

Habitat. Marbled polecats range from southeastern Europe through the Middle East and into western China. Much of their dry grassland *habitat* (living area) is a form of steppe. The grasses there tend to be short and sparse.

Threats. Much of the polecat's steppe habitat in Europe and China has been destroyed by farmland and other human *developments* (activities) since the mid-1900's. Unwise agricultural practices have depleted much of the land of nutrients, turning it into barren desert. Such drastic habitat changes have caused the polecat population to plummet in some areas.

The marbled polecat also faces other human-related problems. Poisons that people put out to kill pests have killed some of the polecat's natural prey. *Poaching* (illegal hunting) has also contributed to their population decline. Road construction breaks up the polecat's habitat and leads to fatal accidents with vehicles.

The polecat is actually a member of the weasel family. Its decline is chiefly the result of habitat loss and destruction.

Mustela lutreola

Conservation status: Critically Endangered

This smaller cousin of the American mink is one of the most endangered mammals in Europe. Although many European mink exist in commercial breeding facilities, wild populations are small. Once common throughout the continent, the wild European mink now exists only in parts of Spain, France, and eastern Europe (Romania, Russia, and Ukraine).

People have long hunted the European mink for its luxurious, blackish-brown winter fur, though its pelt is not as commercially valuable as that of the American mink. Both kinds of mink have double-layered fur. The oily outer layer repels water, keeping the mink dry as it hunts in lakes, rivers, swamps, and marshes. The soft, thick layer beneath keeps the mink warm.

Diet. Minks usually hunt at night. In the water, they hunt for insects, fish, shellfish, crabs, frogs, and water voles (mouselike animals). On land, they look for mice, muskrats, rabbits, and snakes.

Dens. Minks make their dens in or near the water, sometimes in a hole in a stream bank. They line the den with leaves, grass, fur, and feathers. Minks may also take over the burrows of muskrats. They just move in if the burrow is abandoned. But they may also kill and eat muskrats unlucky enough to be at home. Minks travel through large home *ranges* (areas where they live naturally) so they use many different dens over time.

Breeding. Like polecats, minks can be very aggressive animals. Even when males and females mate, the bonding may be accompanied by a large amount of fighting, clawing, hissing, and screaming. The female raises the young by herself in her den. Other than during breeding season, minks spend their time alone.

Threats. Since commercial trapping for the European mink increased in the mid-1800's, the animal's range has declined by an estimated 85 percent. Destruction of their *habitats* (living areas), hydroelectric dam construction, water pollution, and the spread of roads and mink-killing vehicles have hastened the animal's decline.

The greatest problem for the wild European mink, however, has been competition with the larger American mink. In the 1920's, people began establishing mink farms, also called mink ranches, for the American mink in Europe.

Unfortunately, many American minks have escaped from these farms and established wild populations. In fights for food or *territory* (personal area), the American *species* (type) usually wins.

Conservation. Conservationists are working in various ways to save wild populations of this extremely rare and beautiful animal. One effort involves breeding European minks on islands to build up the wild population in locations safe from the American mink.

The European mink has long been prized for its double-layered fur, which keeps the animal warm and dry in the water.

Monachus monachus

Conservation status: Critically Endangered

Since ancient times, people have reported seeing this *species* (type) in the North Atlantic Ocean, the Mediterranean Sea, the Black Sea, and other bodies of saltwater. In fact, some historians believe that ancient legends about mermaids may have been based on hazy sightings of Mediterranean monk seals. The "monk" part of the seal's name is based on the dark fur on the head that looks like the hood worn by some religious men, called monks.

Today, the monk seal is rare. Centuries of slaughter and disturbances of their *habitats* (living areas) have dramatically reduced its populations. The species currently exists only in small, *fragmented* (broken-up) populations in various locations—totaling perhaps 600 individuals. Biologists believe that the largest remaining groups live in the Ionian and Aegean seas, off the coasts of Italy and Greece. Some may live in scattered spots in the southeastern section of the North Atlantic Ocean.

Appearance. Mediterranean monk seals are large, growing to a length of almost 8 feet (2.4 meters) and a weight of 660 pounds (300 kilograms). The color and texture of their fur changes as they age. When they are born, they have woolly fur that is mostly black, with a small white or yellow belly patch. The shape of this patch depends on whether the seal is male or female. The fur become smoother and changes to grayish or brownish in adults. Adult males keep their belly patch, but the rest of their fur may change return to black when they become older.

Social life. Like most other *pinnipeds* (seals, sea lions, and walruses), monk seals are intelligent animals that gather in social groups. These groups are usually small, made up of only two or three individuals. However, larger groups often get together when it's time to *molt*—that is, shed their fur and outer layer of skin to grow new fur and skin. This molting takes place in sea caves, along rocky shores, or on sandy beaches.

Threats. Mediterranean monk seals have long been killed for their meat, hides, and fat, which was converted to oil. In addition, fishers have killed many monk seals because they view the animals as threats to their fish and squid catches. The animals also sometimes drown when they get tangled in fishing lines and nets. The monk seal's habitat—including its molting and nursing sites—has been severely disturbed by human *developments* (activities) along coastlines. Such areas have also been contaminated by industrial pollution.

Conservation. Several international treaties and agreements aim to protect and restore Mediterranean monk seal populations. But some conservationists think it may be too late to save this species.

The Mediterranean monk seal is on the verge of extinction, in large part because it has been hunted for centuries.

Nyctalus azoreum

Conservation status: Endangered

The Azorean bat, also called the Azores noctule, is a small, black bat found in forested and rocky *habitats* (living areas) on the Azores, a group of islands off the western coast of Portugal. Weighing less than half an ounce (15 grams), this flying mammal has tiny eyes and the long ears common to its *order* (group of families).

Hunting. Like many bat *species* (types), the Azorean bat uses *echolocation* to help it find flying insects, its main food source. That is, the bat sends out high-pitched sound waves, which "bounce" off insects and other objects. The returning echoes helps the bat zero in on its prey.

Unlike most other bat species, the Azorean bat hunts during the day. Bats generally hunt at twilight or at night to evade hawks, eagles, and other bird predators—which hunt during the day. Biologists have proposed that the Azorean bat's daytime hunting behavior developed because predator birds don't exist in the Azores.

Reproduction. Female Azorean bats gather in hidden roosts once a year to give birth. These roosts may be inside hollow trees, rock crevices, or buildings. Pregnancy lasts for 70 to 75 days, after which one or two babies are born. The young are cared for until they can hunt on their own.

Habitat. The Azorean bat lives on seven of the nine islands in the Azores. Scientists believe the bat is the only species of mammal native to those islands. Besides its natural habitats, the bat can also be seen flying around streetlights and roosting inside buildings on the islands. Scientists estimate that the total population is from 2,000 to 5,000 individuals, with the largest colony living on the island of San Miguel.

Threats. The purposeful killing of the bats and the destruction of their roost sites by people are the most likely reasons why the Azorean bat has become endangered. The daytime flights of this species make it easy for people to track down its roosting sites. Another reason for the bat's endangered status is the poisoning of its habitats with agricultural and industrial chemicals. Its natural habitats have been further *degraded* (damaged) by the introduction of foreign species of plants. These plants have replaced some of the native plant species that the bat's insect prey rely on for food.

Conservation. Conservationists are seeking to educate the public about the Azorean bat so that people better understand the harm their activities can cause the bat. The main goals of this education campaign include improving the protection of the bat's roosts and restoring its natural habitats.

The Azorean bat (inset), also known as the Azores noctule, has been relentlessly killed by people who wrongly fear the animal. The largest colony of the bats lives on San Miguel Island (background).

Pipistrellus maderensis

Conservation status: Endangered

Like the Azorean bat, the Madeira pipistrelle lives on islands off the coast of Portugal—particularly on the island of Madeira and the western Canary Islands.

Appearance. At 0.2 ounce (6 grams), the Madeira pipistrele is even smaller than its Azores cousin. This tiny, brown bat has short, broad ears. The female is usually larger than the male.

Roosts. The Madeira pipistrelle likes to roost in tree hollows, rock crevices, and other sheltered spots in natural settings. In buildings, it may be found hanging beneath roofs or wedged in other spaces. Sometimes it roosts in bird houses.

Hunting. These bats have a jerky flying style that makes them easy to identify. They are among the first of their kind to appear in the evening skies to seek out moths, flies, and other insects. Like other bats, they rely on *echolocation* (sending out sounds and receiving echoes) to find their prey. They hunt over a variety of insect *habitats* (living areas), including woodlands and farmlands.

As the bats fly, they make a variety of calls to communicate with other members of their group. Some calls are meant to announce their claims to a feeding site and to keep competitors away. Other calls are used to attract mates.

Reproduction. Like several other kinds of bats, female Madeira pipistrelles have delayed *fertilization* of their *eggs* (female sex cells)—that is, the male's *sperm* (male sex cells) does not immediately combine with the female's eggs. Mating takes place in late summer, but the female stores the sperm inside her body during winter *hibernation*. (Hibernation is an inactive, sleeplike state that some animals enter during the winter.) The sperm does not fertilize the eggs until the bats become active again in

spring. This way, the young bats are born and raised in the early summer, when food is abundant and their chance of survival is greatest.

Threats. The Madeira pipistrelle is better than most other bat *species* (types) at surviving in places disturbed by human *developments* (activities). Nevertheless, human activities have caused this bat population to plummet. Habitat destruction ranks as the top reason for this crash. Agricultural pesticides and other *toxic* (poisonous) chemical compounds have polluted many parts of the bat's habitats, likely leading to diseases and deaths among the bats. In addition, people often disturb or destroy the bat's roosting sites inside buildings.

Conservation. Scientists and conservationists are working to identify, monitor, and protect roosts of the Madeira pipistrelle. They are also conducting research to better understand the biology and behavior of this rare little bat. Such actions are extremely important if this species is to be saved from extinction.

The Madeira pipistrelle is under threat from habitat destruction and pollution.

Delphinus delphis

Conservation status: Least Concern

One of the most beloved of all animals, the short-beaked common dolphin is well-known for its intelligence, playfulness, communication abilities, and social behaviors. These marine mammals hunt for fish and squid in large groups, called pods, that may consist of hundreds of individuals. The dolphins are speedy swimmers, moving as fast as 28 miles (45 kilometers) per hour. As they cruise through the open ocean, they can sometimes be seen *breaching* (leaping out of the water) and slapping their flippers on the water surface.

Appearance. The short-beaked common dolphin grows to a length of 8 feet (2.4 meters) and a weight of 165 pounds (75 kilograms). Its grayish body is marked by a unique hourglass-type pattern on the sides. Its snout is shorter than those of the other *species* (type) of common dolphin, the long-beaked common dolphin.

Communication. Common dolphins make a wide variety of sounds. Clicking sounds are used in their echolocation system, in which the *melon* (a fatty organ on their head) directs the sounds forward. The dolphins then listen for the echoes reflecting off objects in their path. This system helps the dolphins to find prey and to navigate through the sea. Other clicks, whistles, and complex sounds are used to communicate with members of the pod.

Habitat. The short-beaked common dolphin is the most common and widespread species of dolphin, with populations found in all tropical, subtropical, and warm temperate seas. However, biologists estimate that the population in the Mediterranean Sea has fallen by more than 50 percent since the mid-1900's. Although the species as a whole is classified as being of "Least Concern" by the IUCN, the Mediterranean population is considered to be "Endangered."

Threats. Scientists do not fully understand why the dolphin is disappearing from the Mediterranean Sea. They attribute part of the decline to a loss of high-quality natural *habitats* (living areas) in the sea. As cities, industries, ports, farms, and other human *developments* have continued to spread across the region, the sea has been increasingly affected by chemical pollution and a problem called *eutrophication*. In such cases, high levels of nutrients in the water from fertilizer run-off and sewage discharge cause an excessive growth of algae. When the algae die, bacteria in the water break them down. This bacterial activity causes oxygen levels in the water to plummet, leading to the death of many fish and other aquatic animals.

Overfishing in the Mediterranean has also depleted some of the fish species that dolphins feed on. In addition, dolphins are killed when they accidentally become entangled in driftnets and other fishing gear.

The short-beaked common dolphin is the most common—and most beloved—of all dolphin species.

Bison bonasus

Conservation status: Vulnerable

The European bison, also known as the wisent, is a major success story in conservation. In the mid-1900's, the wisent was on the verge of extinction. Today, thanks to captive breeding programs, about 1,000 wisents live in the wild. But this great animal still faces many challenges.

Appearance. The European bison is a slightly smaller version of the American bison. Both *species* (types) have a similar body shape, with a large head, curved horns, short neck, and large shoulder hump. But the wisent's head is smaller, and its hump is carried higher.

The largest *bull* (male) wisents are about 9.8 feet (3 meters) long and weigh some 2,200 pounds (1,000 kilograms)—compared to a maximum length of 12.5 feet (3.8 meters) for their American relative. The wisent is the largest *herbivore* (plant-eating animal) in Europe.

Behavior. Wisents and American bison also share certain behaviors. Bulls live in herds with other males. *Cows* (females) live in herds with other females and their young. During the breeding season, the males join the female herds to find mates. The bulls often get into fights as they compete for the cows.

Diet. To support their massive bodies, wisents need to graze on huge amounts of grasses, leaves, shoots, and other plant material. A bull may consume 70 pounds (32 kilograms) of plant matter every day during summer. In some nature reserves, such as the Bialowieza Forest in Poland, workers set out bales of hay for wisents in the winter to make sure that the animals have plenty to eat.

Habitat. The original *range* (natural area) of the wisent covered forests and grasslands in western, central, and southeastern Europe. But by the late 1800's, only two wild populations of these animals remained. One was in the

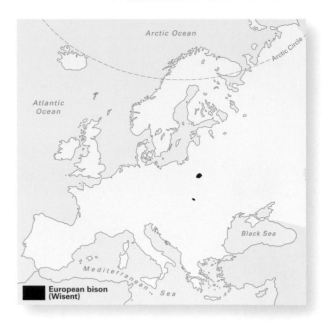

European bison
(Wisent)

Bialowieza Forest; the other was in the western Caucasus Mountains. Both of those wild populations had disappeared by the l920's—leaving only 54 captive individuals in a few zoos.

Threats. The wisent disappeared from the wild because of the destruction of its *habitats* (living areas) from logging and farming activities and because of overhunting. An overpopulation of certain deer species that stripped habitats of plant food also threatened the wisent.

Conservation. Since about 1950, captive-breeding programs—followed by the reintroduction of wisents into the wild—have restored small wild populations in Poland, Lithuania, Russia, and other parts of eastern Europe. Although still small, these populations are increasing under the protection of conservation laws.

Nevertheless, wisents are unlikely to ever exist in large numbers as they once did because available habitat is limited. In addition, the wisent's health as a species has been weakened by disease and *inbreeding* (mating with close relatives). *Poaching* (illegal hunting) also remains a problem.

The European bison, also called the wisent,
was pulled back from the brink of extinction by
captive-breeding programs and legal protections.

Saiga tatarica

Conservation status: Critically Endangered

This *species* (type) was formerly common throughout the *steppes* and semidesert areas of eastern Europe and Asia. (A steppe is a level, treeless plain.) When the Soviet Union existed, authorities carefully managed and protected the saiga antelope herds on land under their control. For example, strict regulation of hunting allowed the species's population to grow. However, the antelope lost much of its protection in the political chaos that followed the collapse of the Soviet Union in 1991, which broke up into separate countries. Since then, the saiga's population has declined drastically.

Appearance. The large tan-colored nose that hangs down over the mouth of the saiga antelope gives the face of this animal an extremely unusual appearance. The nose helps filter out airborne dust from the antelope's dry, cool *habitat* (living area) and it warms the air that it breathes in. The male also has two straight horns marked with rings at the bottom. The animal's fur is mostly a tan-buff color during the warm months, but it changes to white and grows thicker for winter. Males, which are larger than females, range from about 4 to 5 feet (1.2 to 1.5 meters) long, stand about 2 feet (70 centimeters) tall at the shoulders, and weigh from about 70 to 112 pounds (32 to 51 kilograms).

Migrations. Each year, herds of saiga antelope migrate between their summertime steppe grassland grounds and wintertime pastures in semidesert areas farther south. They graze on grasses, herbs, and shrubs. During their migrations, the animals may travel more than 70 miles (113 kilometers) per day.

Reproduction. The antelope mate on their winter grounds, where males collect groups of females, known as "harems." Each male vigorously defends his harem against the advances of other males, and fights frequently break out.

Saiga antelope

Many males die in these violent clashes. In the spring, the herds, including newly born calves, head back north.

Habitat. Saiga antelope are found in scattered populations from southeastern Europe to western China. Biologists have identified four separate populations in Russia and Kazakhstan that travel into Uzbekistan and Turkmenistan in winter. Another population has been identified in western Mongolia.

Threats. *Poachers* (illegal hunters) kill the antelope to get the males' horns, which are sold on the international black, or unlawful, market to make traditional Chinese medicines. The antelope are also poached for their meat. The killing of so many males means that most remaining herds of saiga antelope have too few males for the herds to successfully reproduce. Furthermore, the steppe habitat and migration routes of the species are being destroyed at an increasing rate by roads, canals, and other human *developments* (activities).

Two saiga calves suckle their mother at a nature reserve in Russia.

Glossary

Barbel A long, fleshy, whiskerlike growth.

Biodiversity The variety that exists among different types of animals and plants.

Brackish Slightly salty.

Breaching A behavior in which some species of marine mammal leap from the water and splash back in.

Bull A full-grown male of many large animals.

Conifer A trees or shrub that bears its seeds in cones.

Cow A full-grown female of cattle and related animals.

Crustacean An invertebrate animal with many jointed legs and a hard external shell.

Development Refers to farmland, cities, roads, or other changes that damage the natural environment.

Degrade Reduce in quality.

Dredging Clearing out the bottom of rivers, harbors, and other bodies of water so that ships can use them.

Echolocation A system in which certain animals make a series of sounds and listen for the echoes reflecting off objects to help them hunt and navigate.

Ecosystem A natural system made up of the living organisms and the physical environment in a region.

Egg Female sex cell.

Eutrophication The build-up of nutrients in bodies of water, causing the rapid growth of algae, which deplete the water of oxygen when they die and are broken down by bacteria.

Fertilization In animal reproduction, the union of a male's sperm and a female's egg to form a cell that will develop into a new individual.

Fragmentation The breakup of a habitat, often by human development, into areas that grow smaller and farther apart.

Genus A group of related animals or plants that ranks below a family or subfamily and above a species.

Habitat The kind of place in which an organism usually lives.

Herbivore Any animal that eats chiefly plants.

Hibernation An inactive, sleeplike state.

Inbreeding The mating of closely related individuals.

Incubation The process in which fertilized eggs and young animals are kept under proper conditions for growth and development.

Invertebrate An animal without a backbone.

Iridescent Displaying changing colors, like those of the rainbow, depending on the angle from which the object is viewed.

Larva An immature form of an insect or certain other animals (plural: larvae).

Lek A meeting ground in which male birds gather, display their plumage, and court females.

Melon A fatty organ on top of the head of certain sea mammals that directs sounds forward.

Metamorphosis The extreme changes in form and appearance that occur in lower animals between the growing phase of life and the mature adult phase.

Mollusk A soft-bodied animal that is typically covered with a hard shell.

Molt To shed skin or other growths before new growth.

Nematode A type of slender, unsegmented, cylindrical worm, often tapered near the ends.

Nomad A person who moves from place to place as a way of obtaining food or otherwise making a living.

Order A group of plants and animals that is below or smaller than a class, but larger than a family.

Pectoral fin A fin behind the gill openings of a fish.

Pinniped A group of marine, meat-eating mammals that includes seals, sea lions, and walruses.

Poacher A person who hunts illegally.

Range The district in which certain plants or animals live or naturally occur

Raptor A bird of prey, such as an eagle or a hawk.

Species A group of animals or plants that have certain permanent characteristics in common and are able to interbreed.

Sperm Male sex cell.

Steppe A level, treeless plain in southeastern Europe and parts of Asia.

Talon The claw of an animal, especially a bird of prey.

Territory An area within definite boundaries, such as a nesting ground, in which an animal lives and from which it keeps out others of its kind.

Toxic Poisonous.

Trawling A method of fishing in which a large net is pulled through the water behind a boat.

Urban Of or relating to cities.

Venemous Poisonous.

Vertebrate An animal with a *vertebral column* (backbone, or spine).

Wetland Any area of land where the ground remains soaked with water or submerged beneath water for most of the year.

Books

Hammond, Paula. *The Atlas of Endangered Animals: Wildlife Under Threat Around the World*. Tarrytown, NY: Marshall Cavendish, 2010. Print.

Harris, Tim. *Mammals of the Northern Hemisphere*. Tucson, AZ: Brown Bear Books, 2011. Print.

Hoare, Ben, and Tom Jackson. *Endangered Animals*. New York: DK Pub., 2010. Print.

Silhol, Sandrine, Gaëlle Guérive, and Marie Doucedame. *Extraordinary Endangered Animals*. New York: Abrams Books for Young Readers, 2011. Print.

Weston, Christopher, and Art Wolfe. *Animals on the Edge: Reporting from the Frontline of Extinction*. New York: Thames & Hudson, 2009. Print.

Websites

Arkive. Wildscreen, 2014. Web. 14 May 2014.

"Endangered Species." *BBC Bitesize Science*. BBC, 2014. Web. 21 May 2014.

"Especies Fact Sheets." *Kids' Planet*. Defenders of Wildlife, n.d. Web. 14 May 2014.

European Wildlife. European Wildlife, 2010. Web. 21 May 2014.

Tregaskis, Shiona. "The world's extinct and endangered species – interactive map." *The Guardian*. Guardian News and Media Limited, 3 Sept. 2012. Web. 14 May 2014.

"UK & Europe." *Zoological Society of London*. Zoological Society of London, n.d. Web. 21 May 2014.

Organizations *for helping endangered animals*

Edinburgh Zoo – Adoptions
Adopt endangered animals from Edinburgh Zoo or the Highland Wildlife Park.
https://adoption.edinburghzoo.org.uk/

Defenders of Wildlife
Founded in 1947, Defenders of Wildlife is a major national conservation organization focused on wildlife and habitat conservation.
http://www.defenders.org/take-action

National Geographic – Big Cats Initiative
National Geographic, along with Dereck and Beverly Joubert, launched the Big Cats Initiative to raise awareness and implement change to the dire situation facing big cats.
http://animals.nationalgeographic.com/animals/big-cats-initiative/

National Geographic – The Ocean Initiative
National Geographic's Ocean Initiative helps identify and support individuals and organizations that are using creative and entrepreneurial approaches to marine conservation.
http://ocean.nationalgeographic.com/ocean/about-ocean-initiative

National Wildlife Federation – Adoption Center
Symbolically adopt your favorite species and at the same time support the National Wildlife Federation's important work protecting wildlife and connecting people to nature.
http://www.shopnwf.org/Adoption-Center/index.cat

Neighbor Ape
Neighbor Ape strives to conserve the habitat of wild chimpanzees in southeastern Senegal, to protect the chimpanzees themselves, and to provide for the well-being of the Senegalese people who have traditionally lived in the area alongside these chimpanzees.
http://www.globalgiving.org/donate/10235/neighbor-ape/

Smithsonian National Zoo – Adopt a Species
The Adopt a Species program supports the National Zoo's extraordinary work in the conservation and care of the world's rarest animals.
http://nationalzoo.si.edu/support/adoptspecies/

World Wildlife Fund
World Wildlife Fund works in 100 countries and is supported by over 1 million members in the United States and close to 5 million globally.
http://www.worldwildlife.org/how-to-help

Index

Acknowledgments

The publishers acknowledge the following sources for illustrations. Credits read from top to bottom, left to right, on their respective pages. All maps, charts, and diagrams were prepared by the staff unless otherwise noted.

COVER © Visual&Written SL/Alamy Images; © Erez Herrnstadt, Alamy Images
4 © Erez Herrnstadt, Alamy Images
6 © Emanuele Biggi, Minden Pictures
7 © blickwinkel/Alamy Images
9 © Robert Thompson, Minden Pictures
11 © Gerard Soury, Getty Images
13 © Wil Meinderts, Minden Pictures
15 © Wild Wonders of Europe/Nature Picture Library
16 © Jonathan Plant, Alamy Images
17 © Nature's Images/Science Source
19 © Luis Enrique Minguez Vaquero; © Shutterstock
20 © Chris Mattison, Alamy Images
21 © Jan Van Der Voort
23 © Mark Caunt, Alamy Images
25 © Genevieve Vallee, Alamy Images
27 © David Tipling, Getty Images
29 © Pete Oxford, Minden Pictures
31 © Valdimir Motycka
33 © Sven-Erik Arndt, Alamy Images
35 © Wild Wonders of Europe/Nature Picture Library
37 © Filipe Lopes; © Shutterstock
39 © José Jesus
41 ©FLPA/Alamy Images
43 © Karl Van Ginderdeuren, Minden Pictures
45 © Wild Wonders of Europe/Minden Pictures

Bullard Sanford
Memorial Library
520 W. Huron Ave.
Vassar, MI 48768

591.68   World Book, Inc
WOR   Endangered Animals of
         Europe

DEC -- 2014

DATE DUE

PRINTED IN U.S.A.